SUMMERS OF VIETNAM

SUMMERS OF VIETNAM

and Other Poems

MARY KINZIE

The Sheep Meadow Press
Riverdale-on-Hudson, New York

All inquiries and permission requests should be addressed to: The Sheep Meadow Press, P.O. Box 1345, Riverdale-on-Hudson, New York 10471.

Distributed by Consortium Book Sales & Distribution, Inc.
213 East 4th Street
St. Paul, MN 55101

Design and typesetting by Keystrokes, Lenox, Massachusetts
The book was composed in Mergenthaler Bembo

Library of Congress Cataloging in Publication Data

Kinzie, Mary.
Summers of Vietnam and other poems / Mary Kinzie.
p. cm.
ISBN 0-935296-87-5. — ISBN 0-935296-83-2 (pbk.)
I. Title.
PS3561.I59S85 1989
811'.54—dc 19 89-4116
CIP

Printed in the United States of America

ACKNOWLEDGMENTS

Grateful acknowledgment is made to the following magazines for publishing these poems and for allowing them to be reprinted:

American Review (originally ***New American Review***): *The Brief Against Pluralism*
American Poetry Review: *The Chanticleer; Glad Day*
The American Scholar: *Small Birthday Poem*
Carolina Quarterly: *Stundenbuch; An Engraving of Blake*
Chicago Review: *The Betrothed* (as *In the Queen's Chamber*)
The New Republic: *The Shed; Ringing Words*
The New Yorker: *Reading an Old Poem of Mine; Vulcan*
Overtures (Chicago): *Iseult of Brittany*
Poetry: *Half Rations; The Bamberger Reiter; Nereid's Song; Chagall in His Sickness; The Human Face; The Muse of Satire; Accidie; Superbia*
Salmagundi: *Down to Quantico; At Wentworth-by-the-Sea; Diner; The Palace of Defectives; Days of Darkness; The Charm; When We Turned Our Backs on It, the Ocean; Melisande; A Guide to Fallen Country; To God Who Gets Away with Things; Painting* (as *Van Eyck*); *Allegory*
Sequoia: *Dark Carol*
Southern Review: *Summers of Vietnam; Letter to Portsmouth Naval Prison; Dread* (as *Resurrection*); *Modern Love; Parting Inscription; Ghiberti's Eve*
The Threepenny Review: *Looking into Life*
Yale Review: *On the Actor Edward Petherbridge*

I would also like to thank the John Simon Guggenheim Memorial Foundation for a fellowship that enabled me to compose a number of these poems. M.K.

CONTENTS

I. SEASONS OF VIETNAM

For Jon

SMALL BIRTHDAY POEM

Foggy and dark, this birthday you're
No different than you were when,
Not halfway home, at twenty-four,
You turned my head. Strong as a wave
Stubborn with light; equable; brave;—
Qualities that move me now much more
Than when their force diminished other men.

Heat Lightning

SUMMERS OF VIETNAM

RISING toward New England along the throughway,
The car I drove in alone shot forward
Beneath me, sighing in the echoing return
Of the engine, banked repeating precipice,
Blue mounds of country that made me sigh to see them,
And the thought, which was several thoughts at once:
Again I am alone in the heavy growing
Of the huge, harmless American trees with hands
For leaves. Summer must be hurried to
But disappears before I can arrive.
I have been here before. I have been sent away.
Everything has always shot out from view
Beneath the wheel, my gaze.
Into the towns
Whose stop signs stall me on each hot blue hill,
Baking incline, monastery view,
I stutter through the shining afternoon.
Lives I look at going by, go on
To the end of the thirty-mile-an-hour zone
Where that last filling station has always gone to seed.
Farms start up again, in moons and arrows of field,
Then resume their sweep over quilts of beet, corn, clover,
And, gaining speed, past each clear square field,
The seats melt in the slant of the sun, tar
Wavers to nonsense with its childish patches
Across the pale magma that the road runs to
Through air growing colder by the clock,
Condensing the tarmac, the fields, my face, in fever.

I cannot memorize my license tags.
Each of the visiting days in the "facility"
That looks like a movie lot, placeless, fictitious—
Streets of metal crossed with trolley grooves,

The docks and hangars of heavy masonry,
No trees to speak of, in the air the layers
Of diesel, aftershave, ironed uniforms—
I wait in the sentry room with the other women,
None over thirty, who have come to see the men,
None over thirty, who have killed their commanders
In the loud, unmanning, placeless, fictitious jungle—
The man I come to see refused to go;
They keep him in solitary, the only officer here,
Whom even the guards would like to have extinguished—
And I always have to go outside again
To read the forgotten but over-familiar license
That, like their industry at spreading war
(As if ingrained too deeply in the body
To be summonable by the mind),
Still means nothing, although I recognize it.

As I am cleared, I map in thought the dead
Journey on service roads to tall gates
That will keep me straining to the posted speed;
Reach the rooms with peeling walls and spotless floors
That mirror forward the chairless latitudes
Through which I will halt to see you, under guard;
And I know that such foreboding has never mattered
Less than in these naval yards like cities,
Where those on the ground look the same as seen from the air,
From the deep, from the white cloud on a radar screen,
As everything that does not number, fades.

They bring you in. In pairs, they watch us meet,
Twin Molechs burning everywhere you pass
Lest someone see the hell from which you enter.
One's by the door on his feet. One's in the air,
It seems, lowering. He gets two chairs.
The place is filled by something horrible
Talking cannot dispel, the *tink* of metal.
What you are like is still beyond description.

I don't mean your thin arms, I mean your eyes.
You hum into my hair. I kiss your collar.
They break it up.
                        You say that you are happy
For this test. You say you're teaching grammar
To psychotics and the lesser dead.
You have discovered that Defending Counsel . . .
Your father's death when you were ten . . . your mother's
Operation . . . you've written it all down,
What you learned, what you must now renew.
They break it up again *(What a conversation!)*
Until tomorrow,
                        when two different demons,
Who will do their job, at barely twenty,
Much better than they need, won't see us weep
When we join what is not parted for another week.

As they take you out, I map in thought
Your hours of solitude, what you won't eat
And will not see, in that half-assembled
Country of the past where I don't travel.
For myself, the real reduces to
The pads of explanations you write in code
And the line from Portsmouth to Baltimore,
Which I think of in the small, seen from a distance—
How close my going puts me to coming back—
Until I am nothing unless I am in motion
Across a land that has no time for me.
You float above lost time, I race against it,
Until we are like those places seen only from the air
At high speed, without transition from street
To field, from fiat and thrift to the aimless fears—
Non sequiturs—imbedded in the given,
Which deepen long after we have passed them by.

GRASSHOPPER

At this moment, however, the wine dreggy and the cheese slick
With oil, the skin allergically prickling in
The swathes of green hay, we were untouched by time.

You belonged to me, the image of my passions. All of nature
Strove about your head (as I strove, armed in quiet, urgent
With awe I hoped to fan to new infection

At how I made you feel), as if to catch your beauty by its breath,
Match your ardor with its own—although it thrashed, fretted, sinking
Into redundancy, fitful in fitful swoons, awaking like a bird

That darts its spindle of slick feathers into the wood, there
To close its wings down on a thorax gleaming like a fuselage,
Its eyes blinking in points of electric light.

Beneath the closed dome of a mountain heat wave,
The thought of bed cool and heavy, like white mist on the tarn,
We scared up long brown grasshoppers coated with membranes

Of dust and flecked with chaff. Their wings, veined olive,
Brushed the tops of the powerful dun thighs. One
Lit on a stalk, eyeing us. But the stalk

Was another insect and the gaze, one of irony and impudence.
You shook your leg; another tumbled out from under the cuff
Then spat into the road.

The dust in the tire ruts was coiled
With grasshoppers, the field a mat of clicking through which they broke
When they flew, and although the prospect held its shape
In general, each corner of the meadow where we have lain

Boiled into chaos, beneath our shadows foaming like flood water
   Into excited conduits
      Of insects jostling in all directions below an eerie light

Whose static blue grated with the blank severe
   To which it would continue to subject us.

We looked on this
Like children, confident that to the great, because benevolent,
   All power was sweet, and to be turbulent—implacable—
      Were transitory emanations

Precipitated from the laden sky as from excess of charge.

READING AN OLD POEM OF MINE

How much of what I did then was unhealthy.
Smoking when I woke up, until I dropped
At day's end, fidgety and bottled up
Like something on the edge of overripeness,
Into a drowse of wanting. All was want.
Want of youth—I did not have enough
To make the lines I had not thought through yet
Pierce the surface and reverberate.
I must have formed some idea of a public.
Or the want of you—we ate and breathed the same,
Closer we could not be, even our quarrels
Bore the sly stamp of how to make them up—
But the same fire lacked in this. So we fought again
Until the want of industry to fight
Laid us out like children on the bed,
Yawning and sodden, your profile flickered at
By the heat lightning that used up all the air,
And still the want of oxygen, and the cigarettes,
And the summer night that had not any future,
And the powerful bodies we could use any way
Tried to get on the page, and could not. It's all there.

THE CHANTICLEER

"... trewely she hath the hert in hold
Of Chauntecleer, locken in every lith.
He loved hir so that wel was him therewith."

—Chaucer, "The Nun's Priest's Tale"

I STILL have the unredeemed
Large sunbright pasteboard tickets
To the complicated late
Basie, not as weird as Miles
Nor friendly as Ellington
But sheer like the Aztec stone
The victims scarcely noticed
Bleeding them (which does not last).
For once the Famous Ballroom
Had drab bookings so great jazz
Poured out to *our* neighborhood
From a place we had not seen,
So near, so small, so like a
Hole-in-the-wall corner bar
Where a skittish rooster pecks
The dirt in Middle English—
   He gan gronen in his throte
   Chuk chuk to his Pertelote
(Borges would have had it speak
In Creole forms of Latin
No one had hear of)—as if
America had fallen
Away and the Spanish shores
Lapped against the foot of town,
Poor and spirited.
                                        Spotlit
By its speciality
The wee nightclub crowed in flame

Near the fogbound Chesapeake,
Dwarfing the steep row houses
Like a cartoon of viewpoint
Or of the new soul's rising.

Then bad dreams seemed to loosen
From their chronic symbolism:
You would not
Be roughly seized
In the shed, buried in dung,
Capsized under a clear sky,
Turned over by unseen teeth,
But would live, wish of my flesh,
Locken in every lith.

That night, they arrested you.
Oh Christ, nor when they had gone
Could I endure and watch one hour,
Waiting to hear where you were.
All the lights kept blazing on
In the apartment. Far off
The cock crew and crew and crew
Its subtle redundant riffs
Plunked at by a piano
Ribboning out at daybreak
Like small mermaids' merriment
To slip voiceless down the sea.

When I woke, I felt drunken
And empty of will, burned down
To the flesh I had indulged.
Although from then on I slept
On the floor—even my one
Visitor, quite ill, denied
The solace of our dry bed—
That afterecho of unkindness
Could not bring Count Basie back

For the last set nor yet
Let me, at my window, see
If from the colfox's mouth,
Spurred by some sweet cleverness,
Deliverly the cok brake.

SHUTTLE AND THORN

To my sister

THAT fierce July she bent over her work like another artless
Dornauszieher,
The chimaera of the young Greek boy Aschenbach saw absorbedly
Prising a thorn
From his foot. Hair in dark tongues that trail entangling
Emphases
Over the garish colors of the rug she has rudimentarily
Designed
And is now making—green watermelon with a purple rind,
Pink seeds,
White bordering—the girl blisters her elegantly shaped hand
On the metal punch
With which she drives the damp rug yarns into the stiff
Hairy hemp.

Then one day, more reflective still of the resemblances
Of which
She is unconscious, she coils over the miniature shuttle
Her irksome
Coltishness had sheered off the wooden floor of my room
On Eager Street.
It has driven far into the sole, curled in supplication,
Weaving
In and out her flesh. The doctor, all of his frustrated
Disdain
Of the young bristling in the rebuff, brusquely refuses
To examine it
Until she has washed both limp, bare, narrow, grime-
Polished feet.

To her first tetanus shot as a young woman she responds
In the vein
Of this treatment with acrimony, then with delirium,
Her eyes
Long ringed with lilac from absorbing the vaccine.

DOWN TO QUANTICO

I FELT like a pilot bringing down the wounded
To the base where you were first interned.
Shifted from Baltimore, my sister lay in the back
Looking so ill I would pull off the parkway
To hold her in my arms. But with the rising heat
Flickering in the leathery, dry groves,
The comfort did no good, and I was tardy.

Manic with chastisement and foreboding,
Sluggish in speech and yet incapable
Of quiet, you were like a poisoned animal,
Itself ailing as it grieved around its mate.

★

At the motel, just-furloughed corporals
With harlequin tans and Hare Krishna heads
Crashed down into the chlorinated pool.
In the air conditioning we ate
Steak and pink tomato. I drank gimlets.
Barbie called the ogling fellows skinheads
Who watched her baste all next day by the pool.

Bright as a nail, you told me how your screw
Trained dogs. He lodged in their raw beef throat-thick
Starbursts with bluntened prongs like a child's jack
"To lay off the kill." In return, you lent him *Gordon Pym*.

★

He let us out at dusk to a hacked meadow,
The air like turpentine. We felt the reins
And turned back from each empty patch of time

Into another aimlessness that stuttered.
A school of gnats expiring in a column
Parted and closed around us. Never alighting
But to breed, not eating till they died.

You have begun to doubt your principles,
Conjecture, refutation. Just as well.
Those who swim the twilight of their captors
Break into pieces far too small to see.

LOOKING INTO LIFE

At a curve in a New Hampshire highway,
Neither town nor country, the cropped green
Flush to the asphalt flares up with the color
Of hope against a house, compact and clean.

In the kitchen, down a wooden hallway,
A woman goes back and forth. Her legs are bare
And firm and show a stubble. On the table,
Cucumber, corn, tomato, early pear.

The room is glowing with a hot wet light:
The basket foamed with laundry, the long spoon
Striking into the pot, her moistened forehead,
The produce for the stand that afternoon

That will be pyramided near her child's
Erratically hopeful lettered sign,
"Corn and !!! Cukes"—the letters getting smaller
Near the edge, where "e" and "s" incline—

All glisten with a strong aesthetic glare.
I can't imagine what is on her mind
Or in what form death sniffs around her heels.
When she hems clothes, does she think of mankind?

She is so different I think she must be
Sad like the rain: The sources of dismay
Spring elsewhere than her life. In the flesh, too,
She looks much older, stricken, in a way,

And yet clearer than me, beloved, "resolved,"
Like an over-subtle picture or sweet song

Loosened at last from its disfigured style
And sped toward its object all along.

Call this thing Grace, Simplicity, Belief.
One law has helped the ivy to the wall
And her to cling to truth. Let the war rage.
The screened door takes the breezes down the hall.

I look one second into her closed life,
Rich or poor as it in fact may be,
And, close to tears in mine, pretend to ask,
Would I trade lives with her? would she with me?

LETTER TO PORTSMOUTH NAVAL PRISON

I AM going through your papers once again.
Kenya tea is brewing in the snouted pot.
Dull half-moons of inexpensive onyx
Sulk in bland and blond striations on
A brown rush tray. Such objects speak,
As if aware of me, with the bald and ritual
Gaze of talismans. The envelopes
Have eyes and tongue me "Mary. Mary. Mary."
Bright blinds observe. The demon lengthy bodies
Belonging to friends hover, perfumed and nude,
Beloved of Eakins. Faithless, real distractions.
Bathers in clever paintings near brown ponds.
Men who'd nothing better to do that season.
Unarrested, unimprisoned, undeceived
(One meditates) by water, sun on skin,
Or governments, thus countrymen who'd found
No better congregate than torpid, summer
Nationhood to pin allegiance to. Men
Who would bow to duty in a griping, tawdry war—
Men of the literature. Your mates at reveille,
Courts Martial, manoeuvres, and collective
Manly type of peremptory readiness.
I am going through your papers once again,
But figures are at hand. Betraying. Understood.

Here is the letter that you wrote on Poe,
On that flesh-eating gull in *Gordon Pym*.
Here, summaries of what the sudden stillness
Of the stag in Kierkegaard, the manic
Safety measures of the burrower
In Kafka, and the shattering appeal
Of the disciple that his god "Help Thou
Mine Unbelief" have had to do with you—

Since all will have so much to do with you
As time goes on contracting and you toil
To reconvene your past. You are that child
Who knows the world considers him at night.
Bones growing with great calor under stars
That shudder, rise to wrath, deceive, you
Safely yield your childhood self to sleep,
Dreaming of shouts and water and technical words.
The world solicits you for time to seem,
Who never changes in its colored pools.

You were at center. You are center still.
In a hand so small as to lack characters
You draft benign symbolic codes to mark
Each arbitrary point of your long sleep
As history and absolute. Each man
And willing girl and April funeral
Come, necessary now, and final as inscribed.
You keep revising numerated schemes
For fixing origins of knowledge; ends; release
From Portsmouth where Marines who went berserk
Below Da Nang have worshipped you, their addled
Hermit-priest, you starving, faithful mage.
You do not make sense. Nor can I hope
But that you do.

To comfort the imprisoned
Is impossible. I walk between
Two rooms and touch the pottery, the teak,
A stone owl I once hurled against the floor,
The door. I am not going anywhere. I fear
The city and the bell. At twilight, wounds
And drunken arguments attended by
Police administer the hours until day
And frame the wringing night in local war.
Every voice except for yours has eyes
With which I am seen. Window, envelope,

And stone, and tray, grin their shabby, conscious
Treaty with the street. I answer prose
I barely comprehend for what it meant,
But see, misgiving, what it surely means.
Haunting, lithe betrayers, who are full
Of life, of common sense, and of conscripted
Risk—those Sentencers who give their entire
Unbelief for glory and who always
Win—are ordinary here in your despite.

OLD PORTSMOUTH

SWIFT, illegible signs
Badge side streets narrow
With unforetold turnings,
But recognized, once more,
Like setting in a dream.

A tiny bridge keeps clattering
Over some brackish damp
Curled back on its seeping
Through mazed thicket and cinder-path

Until water broad
Water froths beneath
Pocked pylons and a causeway
Fastens the shores.
There,
The promontory. Sideways
Along, the heroic veranda,
Rocking chairs like thrones
For ogres. The wood façade
Creased minutely like a face
Asleep against the palm.

On the fir-framed putting-green
A Dutch red windmill
Stiff from birth
Miniaturized the view . . .
All this obese Victoriana
Bruising the swatch of land
On which it civilly trod.

AT WENTWORTH-BY-THE-SEA

Pastorale

FRINGED with the firs' young topmost growth, the pair
Of servant's windows looked down, oblique, sparkling,
As if through lashes. By their means, one saw
Time's azure area forlorn, and with their yearning
Moved upon the large and open view
Till it, too, cramped in irritation. Tucked along
A narrow hall at the back of the hotel
Where all the corridors inclined a few degrees
Upward, the tininess of the room lent it
An air of excited thrift. It would attract the Brontës
But for the sloping ceiling's nervous height.
The floor, too, fell a bit so that the windows seemed
To draw like gleaming magnets. (The girls would clasp
Each other at the waist and circle the black, rooted
Furniture, dainty and colorless as moths.)

Beneath them where the promontory lapsed, nothing
Of Wentworth was visible, only the glinting bay
And, on its far side, a deserted shore, which both
Mirrored one's isolation, and emptily
Averted its gaze. Through that smocking of dark boughs,
One glimpsed, far off, the most fantastic building
Rather like a Moorish fairy palace in a book
Of children's tales, offering a cruel vista
Of release set in a land where no one ever
Cried, in destitution, "Make me neat!
Make me neat!" and where in gratitude and silence
Unseen minions did their shining work.

Whitewashed arch and comic stucco cornice and a hint
Of colonnade receding met the eye
With a crystalline shock no path or tendril came to soften;

The contrasts, wilfully extreme. In the brunt
Of light, bright rondure, black recess were whispered back
From their severity only by
The screen of gauze, like a long net for badminton,
That looped down, white as the wet, steep, white lawn.
It gave the sense, the sun along one side, of wicker work.
But then the wind blew and a cloud would brood
Low toward it, and the cross-hatch loosened like tall grass.

In some lights, it resembled spider's gossamer.

Perhaps it was not until late afternoon, my first visit with you cut short by delays and these, teased out by every checkpoint corporal, that I realized there were several of these lines of netting, like veils wrapped around the approach to a pleasure spa, or banks of rippling banners at an outdoor fair. But amid that gay extravagance, the silence, or what lay under it, the isolation, was foreboding. And then, rashly but inexorably, before my eyes, the scene flexed. With the technical polish of a machine, with the expensive lubrication of the humming, smooth teeth of gears, the scene leaped from its repose, bringing near what was far and wistfully minute. In that leap, that seizure, the quaint became sinister. The truth breathed.

It coarsened the weave of the veil, hardened the threads as they grew heavier, too heavy to bear, and rooted the scallops in a mineral stubbornness that stemmed their billowing. The net was really neither cloth nor willow, nor was it spun by spider or silkworm, and instead of making several idle sweeps across the grounds as it drifted from the Moorish dwelling to the rough shore, the gauzy barrier was an unbroken and unbreakable, chain-linked, deeply-planted-on-pylons, barbed, and electrified fence, bound three times at exact intervals around what was—it could, I saw, be nothing else—the Portsmouth Naval Prison.

Geometrical

Neither then, nor ever
Was it granted to see
—Not in all the late days
I huddled at these eyes
Straining to pierce
The myriad apertures
—Never did anyone appear
Burning in the chute
Of light from a window
Nor did living beings
In garments and flesh
Walk along the steep
Yard floored with cubes
Of shadow or patrol
The perimeter. Not
One dog or bird
Ruffled the vacancy.
Even terns disdained
To pick along the scree.

Et Excrucior

The very ground dead as the moon,
The giddy clouds, surreal and mean,
Rocking above the pert lagoon
Where sailboats darted—the whole scene
A mess of styles patched by a ghost
With low-browed grinning and excuse:

This was a prison, in abuse
Grounded and to crime transposed
And slovenly compounded. Ill-
Rehearsed and shabby the façade.
Vacant windowsill and quad.
Not one villainy on drill.

Shamed by a nerveless discontent
I see myself shown up; bereaved;
Consigned to nurse you undeceived
For two decades . . . but kept indifferent.

Outrage had dried back the tear
Too pure to fall, and made it cheap.
It is pride that balks at too-severe
Discouragement. I would not weep,
Gazed off when punished, sworn to sleep
When broken, to the far when near.

DINER

I

Obvious" was what I seemed to myself,
Like the leprous saint in a whole crowd,
Her shift radioactive, her lank hair
Risen in tough shocks like a farm maid's—
Though I had not her flare for aimlessness,
Unselfconscious on the pyre with nothing
In her hands. Even as a game
I could not still my gaze so it expired
Upon its object.
                    Clamped against the world
Rigid, I moved like a hinged monster,
Every word coerced by its prosthesis,
Each outlook forecast, even the view
Crazing itself against the eye that saw it,
The burin crude and mordant, while old plastic,
Sprinkled with something in the silver diner,
Took one's skin against it: Even pleasure
Fastened to the body, like a curse.

II

I had seen this diner, one of those long cars
Uncoupled from an ageing Zephyr, gutted,
Then set down in a pine wood off the road . . .
I hid there like a passenger on fire
Whom no one must see. Beyond me the bright spruces,
Each one smoky with identity,
Charcoal pine cones gored with cavities,
Long brooms of needles shaking with bright gum,
Pinned me to the moment lest it slip my mind
That Time was—Lord, a dull and tortuously
Brutal servant, who would not look away,
His grains made precious as at the hour of death,
That is, they had the value of the void.

Indulgences I came here to forget
Our trouble in—meat from a crusted grill
Anonymously served, the gusts of rancid
Grease and salt smudging the piney air—
Were neutered in the look of those gray needles
Blued by the sun in the seconds palpable
And slowed till even the dust that webbed the fardels
Glinted with arrogance.

The food sank in my body. My throat closed.
My hands looked helpless and familiar. Mindless
Buoys huffed metallic, in the distance.
As the world ground down about my soul,
You were slipping further from me
Into your ordeal. I saw it, eloquent
With hue and tone and shape, and grooved with shade,
Like the fallen cones, with what would come to change us
To heaps of long-untouched, precise debris.
What would I do without you for the rest of time?

III

Compared to pain, the shame of too much pain
Disclosed was just a buzzing at the edge
Briefly rising in the social silence,
Dining at Wentworth. An outsider here,
Whose visit was no holiday; whose yearning,
Which she tried to hide, was evident,
Surely, as if her groin and breasts darkened
The clothes she wore like pulp before it lights;
Who had not learned to occupy herself
And had no charm . . . I watched the waitresses
Glide across the noisy wooden hall,
Pale bass-green eyes efficient but unspeaking,
Hair like wet, new wheat, fruit-colored lips,
Fresh, strong, pale, tall, long-shanked, meticulous,
Whose souls life would not touch, though they had souls
And wished to give them over to a cause.
College girls who worked for Congressmen,
Demonstrated in the parks, opening
Wide those wet, bright mouths as they were carried
To the wagons by two visored men.

Their gestures made me cringe. My mouth was closed.
But if they looked more closely, they would learn
Some things that were not taught about the war.

THE PALACE OF DEFECTIVES

I

SENTENCED for life. Men
Whose confidants had been
Combat dogs, now reassigned.
Their grief, inestimable. The men's,
So deep it rose against
The surface by a trip-wire. Men,
You understand, who would pay
Twice for the tiny whores,
The second time as mounts
For their German shepherds.

II

Hygiene, order, drill.
The food was treated. Long halls
Pallid with reverberation
Led to flaking antechambers
With nothing to them. Day
Ran twice as long. The lungs flat.

Therapeutic works erupted
Scorched with haste yet not one
Scrawling or crude hammered jar
Or view of the tropical veldt
By anyone over the mental age of 12.

III

The palace of defectives
Thin as willow whips, fat as herds,
Inert (stored energy)
Fast-heavy atoms cocked
To leap excitably, and fit
Despite the pyrotechnic
Drugs popped in like seed
To kill when uncommanded.

This, itself, greased a bit
The locked cogs of law:
Enough derangement for obedience
To shine down niggardly into the hold
Like errant glints off metal.
What held them rapt was war.

The guards walked both sides
(They had been there, too)
And kept it all kicked in

Just as long as the prisoners let them do
Their number, in the dark.

THE SHED

"These sacrifices have been offered
by men now living."
—Frazer

We would not need them for another year,
The scarecrow with the beaten metal jaw,
Its straw already dark and smelling bad.
Blades too fine for cutting what we grew.
Pottery at which no one would look,
So negligibly stubby and obtuse
It seemed, like any family's daily ware.
Racks that turned by rudimentary gears
Sprocketed grotesquely, like a game
That would not serve to haul or thresh or sow
But would be halting in the illustration
Of laws by which the heavy were brought low.

An insect-humming made these objects fierce,
As if they knew us and could spur sensation—
However long we put off their abuse,
With which our shadowy grain would overflow—

And then we could not look at the tall frame
Which, at planting, through our nightmares drew,
Many-armed as Shiva, glinting the hook
That brought the victims often on our shears.
Parts of them were growing near the shed.

Which was illusion? To see someone whose
Life last year was swift, now blind or lame
Or self-castrated, and wish he were not dead?
Or was that empty shed a hesitation
On the edge of truth, where god would reappear
Only among the rubbish and taboo

Of the human husk?

If shame is what we know,
In some way, when the next red season nears
And arrows weep down hard on the dead muck
Till we are fearful of the seed we strow
And horns whine in our ears and a tensed bell
Jangles till the piteous senses swell
And we are called to vent the breast's great well,
Our own, or someone's, in the same salvation,
When the old scarecrow works her sweetening maw,
I wonder who among us will withdraw?

Days of Darkness

MIDWINTER

We seem to be dining
Yet the salver offers
Only the unstirred flame
Of the candle whose wax
Melts over my fist.

The plates look wrong
Like circus props
Flaunting their tipsy humor.

Beyond the cloth the gloom
Hardens the air
On which a tired head
Might strike
And reawaken.

You will not look up
To favor the images
Of my remorse—the scum
Of courage. My yearning
Plenteous, sincere
Shrinks you down
Into another surface
Turned away, which says,
The earth is iron
And I am marked for death.
Then I feel my throat
Close up with tears.

By day
A patch of snow in the yard
Flares out, as if a lump of radium
Were sending its dolor
Into the material darkness.

GROUND ZERO

I

Now the cold has shaken all the dust
Out of the empty blue. As if the seal
Were broken, space
Pours into the gaps between life and life.
Their arms compact against their sides,
People walk reluctantly, bent
Like tree limbs, driven by the cold into
The drafty red-brown buildings up long stairs
Where they may be imagined for a moment
Relieved when they hang a coat upon a peg
And their breath does not frost. But when they turn,
The dirty windows funnel down the light
And they must face the same vague noise and random
Cramp of emptiness.
Under the ragged acres
Of rooftops with jutting coping mossed with tar,
Their life will fume away. Blunt chimneys draw
The filmy bolts of smoke into a void
That swallows up these wisps and streaks of white
As if they had not been. Through the brief day,
Many times relentless as the sun
Moves over the far, lisping pastel world,
The fast lacy breaths of the chimneys exhale in haste
Till everything that courses with heat and blood
Is cancelled down to zero,
Leaving the landscape clear and miniature
Like painting done on china.

II

From the tenth floor of a building near the ghetto,
The palette of the city seems to darken
From the blond hard stone, clear glass, and sheer slick metal
To the old reds and livery browns of Maryland.
As if a shadow started here on M Street,
Deepening its inclination toward the east,
Those who drift are stained like winter berries.
In woven coats and dried-out leather caps,
The colored people travel in their gloom,
Gathering to themselves a dim penumbra
Like a light bulb in a faded entry.
The very bricks must bear this atmosphere
Of sepia and maroon out to the daylight
Where the dull brass newel posts and marble stoops
Glimmer like teeth and the fillings in teeth
In expressions uninterpretable.

The snow is hard, faded, dirty, secret
As if recoiling from the darkened gullies
Rounded by the constant tread of feet.
In empty lots and the few once-planted beds
Weed and tree branch clatter woefully
Like something turned into old cardboard,
Which cannot freshen with the rising sap.
One barely hears them, tapping at their husks.
Three miles southwest, tier over tier
In cubicle and office bay, the state
Hums forward through its fertile calculations:
One cannot hear anything. From this remove
Everything is quaint, dry, dreamy—
Except that anyone may own it now,
This toylike isolation, this ground zero.

III

The eye composes the scene into a picture
Until the great blue/pink abyss of sky
Is the cold shell of the self, pressing the buildings
Out to a patterned winter at the margins
As they line up like so much blackened stubble.
Even what is irreducible,
The human, squirming up from the odd corner,
Composes to an ornament or accent—
Something interesting to watch a moment,
Shape and color glazed with a purity
Fallen from the day star—the vaporous wisps
(Prettily pausing before forgetfulness
Wipes away the threads of their existence)
A part of the very rhythm of one's watching,
As are those small black curls like curls of hair,
Which thought curls into reminiscingly,
Or the tired brown stogy woven with firm ash
That lies there on its side, bobbed by the wind.
Later, it will puff out beyond the roof lines . . .

IV

Only in time will one begin to link
The forming plumes of charcoal marbled with cream
To the methodical scurry of cars and people.
In time, their little hub will start to turn,
But awkwardly, in hidden composition
Like water around a stone: With a hurrying nod
Of reverence, they will curl down at this crux,
Or like a wave of insects crossed back by their fellows
Above a kill, whelmed in their own acids—
All so clumsy, and gradual as nature.
Then, like the carbon of a Brueghel, some men will pull
At a stump in the sidewalk—

                                                  a hydrant that has frozen,
And there, all at once, a shiv of orange
Will slit up through a filthy tangle of soot
And one will see the fire, hot, lethal,
Whole in a viciousness that will not stay put,
That tears away at the very rag of particles
It has destroyed already—which was an attic,
Wallpaper, bed, doll, book, cloth, cap, wood, ink—

Yet it will be so far away, one smiles.

DAYS OF DARKNESS

GRIEF, grief. I had forgotten
The shrunken frame, the rancor.

His cranium bears the gaze, abrupt
Or supplicating, with such statuary
Size—so Jehovan, or seraphic—
One forgets the fallen away
Body, the small sinew. One looks
Directly past the sunken works
To the enemy between us,
What has been left
On the tablets which he reads
And slowly emends in mind,
Each stutter of time
Perfectly fixed for interrogation
When he hales it up at a flash:
Need this have been so?

It is worse than losing him.

KNIGHT AND DEATH

SUM of virtue, with a noble heart
Made pliant in the long forge of his will,
At once commander of his mind and too kind
For its heresy of rigor (*Reason
Will think anything*—his motto),
Not immodest of the freedom of his reach
From scarlet state, to fieldcamp, to the sky—
Although, set free of their drifting allegory,
Stars at times appeared to him to sink
Their pinpoints in a waste
Of drearisome enormity:
Why did the clerics take his praise
And then insist the vein should still be severed,
As Nero asked Lucan? Only madmen severed
Future from present so irrevocably,
Or something in the rancor of their rule
Twisted into a feint of policy—
A hatred of restraint that was not cruel,
Mistrust of mouths not coarsened by the bit
Yanked in their sleep to lead them over rubble—
So madness in the small and slow of heart.

Yet seeing him, one knew it was pure envy.
His person, as it met and turned aside
And made to radiate and shed the light
More molten on his subject, made of him
At once the shining creature, blessed and clean,
In whom this beauty hummed,
                                        and a divided
Being, stretched out on his skeleton
By a power he did not approve.
Glinting with cuisse and greave his leg, his torso
Vivid with articulated muscle

And faint with short blond hairs invisible
Until a breeze lifted the air, were not
Devoted to their own regard. (His body
Merely helped him climb where he could see this.)

So, surely, something of his disdain—
Not for the creatures who were drawn to him,
Rulers, children, animals, old women—
But (a little) toward what we admired . . .
When the theme was raised . . . occurred to him
Only in passing. Not caring in the same
Key with the same fervor for the flesh,
The swoon through which it freed itself to pleasure,
Yet he gave in to it, the indulgence
Was a healthy thing and cost him nothing.
Even in moderation an excess
Streamed out from him as on a ray of lightning,
Dragging the senses open as if this
Had chosen him from everything on earth
Until he was hated for not having wished it.

So the very balance of austerities
Their sermons teetered on was, in the deed,
The play of those who spoil, and fear, the flesh.
The frowning world shut down the air around him
An iron and unbreathable disorder
Shone like winter sun on his winter strength.
Even I, who try to memorize it,
When I see the modelled robust chest
Mark the runnels ridden by the future
Into his smooth skin, now shocked and ashen.
Instead of the slim scallops breathing near
The solar plexus, deep ribs have come forth
Like gills that open on his body's dark

Where all is want, and madness. Through his vigor,
As through a disguise, I see his vow
Cancelled, the address to tasks, the force
To clasp and stride and kneel, dropped, pitifully, away
Until his stillness is a kind of fleeing.

Courtliness, encouraged by that arm;
Kisses poured out over the large mouth;
Voracity, prompted and rewarded
By a voice like golden meal . . . across this banquet
Glorious with desire appear the harrows,
Solitude, privation, desuetude,
Breaking down the web of light and water,
Bone, and salt, and sand, into stiff matter
And a few secretions.
                                        In a handful of years
After swift and concentrated hardship,
He would be dry as a winter berry
Over whom the birds contend.

DARK CAROL

> "And lust is forster with his bow and flane;
> Fro tree to tree he chasis me in the nicht."
> —old ballad

LIKE a puppet in her bed,
Away from her he hung his head.
    The wind, blown black about the sky,
    Bough, roof, and drift would magnify
    With angry banding, like the eye
Of something blazing and yet dead.

Though nothing sounded in the air,
Tears fell into her neck and hair,
    The attitudes of their excess
    Concealing a lone brokenness
    That took up joy and made it less
Till they were not warmed anywhere.

Yet there was no climactic "turn."
Time went about the place. The fern
    Took water. They ate down their food.
    Refreshment worked. Their habits stood.
    They practiced being kind and good
And watched the fire creak and burn.

But in their dreams the earth would burn.
Guilt had sealed off their return.
    Dark, tiny creatures like wet leaves
    Seared where they sucked. By enemies
    Observed to tear and bleed and freeze,
Their nightmares made them taciturn.

Elusive grew the profound dark
Where, through the vague, contorted park
    Until their limbs melted like rain,
    The forster with his bow and flane
    Pursued them like corrosive pain,
Shooting upon their sluggish mark.

Still, in the morning, like a charm,
His torso sought out by her arm,
    Her back by his, they waited for
    The furnace to kick in, the door
    To show the first streaks of the ore
That helped to make their bodies warm

That they forget what they could not repeat
In the smooth envelope of each one's heat.

HALF RATIONS

He did not sweat. Even in hot weather
His skin breathed off only a little dew,
The rigorous exhalation of a star,
What is more, it was willed. One felt this.
Concession to the heated exercise
Of life, conducted without greed,
Silently: In everything, three-quarters
Turned away, as in a photograph
I have, lest we be blinded by
His misery and by the mind that looked
Relentlessly upon it
Only in passing.

Calculating what
He would need to eat to stay alive,
Making sure he took in that at the least,
Somehow he slipped entirely into the habit
Of eating *only* that, the minimum
The limit. The quarter-cups of walnuts
Mixed with raisins, honey occasionally,
Cole slaw and potato salads with two eggs,
Apples with a thumb of peanut butter
On each slice. Carrots. Tuna in water.
Yet he looked rucked up like cloth
In which a subtle gather has been taken.

When times were grim between us, he would say,
Please come back to me, I cannot do
With less than I have. So our haggard love
Nourished him a little, all he needed,
The need that found enough in him to want.

REQUIEM

I. *Christmas*

THE Betty Patterson Specialty Kitchen, Baltimore:

So read the sign over a clean shop full of murmuring
   Patrons in dark fatigues on whom streamed the oblique sunlight,
Twilight pale, like the onset of a partial eclipse of itself,
   Who took up and crooned over the shining gifts—soft candies
Wrapped side by side in pretty tins, preserves in diminutive jars
   Of glass with white enamel lids, and crocheted coverings
To cup the feet and hands on a midnight of near repose.

   In the design of the shop, there was no crowding up
Of wares nor urge to rush against the appetite: Vacancy
   Assumed the blessed maternal demeanor of the past
Recalled far on. There were few things but, as in memories,
   Each existed in a substantive and eternal way.

II. *Easter*

As the ladies baked only six or seven kinds of good at times
  Trays behind the single counter of tall glass would lie
Spotlessly bare. A few of the things I found hard, like food
  In a doll's house. But the great confections were always
Perfect in plenitude, new minted in imagination like the round
  Angel food cakes the size of raised biscuit domed with half
Again their height in lemon frosting the hue of the gauzed
  Over sun to which time gave a thin tightening of crystallization;

These were often savored in the ghostly air outside when promise
  Flared about the body with the last convections of attachment
And the wind's tooth was withdrawn. It seemed the wrong thing,
  To eat there in the place, even though an "area" had shaped itself
Near the glinting tea tins and the jam jars in pyramids of six
  Where two Colonial rockers awaited those worn out with waiting
Or who first required to pause
                                        (thus the image leaned sadly out
  From the background)
                                    nodding over their hands, before climbing
Down again into the dried out seasonless barren heavy street.

III. *St. John's Day*

Baltimore was sunk in its swamp of punishments
  But in the little shop the air was soft as a star
Falling from inestimably far until it shone a little
  On the foredoomed as if to try their sorrow. Alone in space
With the empty rocking chairs near the few, odd offerings
  Glowing with self-effacement and a note of gay if quiet
Gerontological humor that would not save their lives—
  What drew them here? —the slight boys briefly stateside—
Nostalgia for the cosmos they would soon be stolen from
  Once they set the jungle aflame?
                                        Betty Patterson herself
(Who else could this have been) was a Luciferian form
  Of limbs wrapped in forest dyed shimmering *Dirndl* cloth,
Her fine hair fluffed out by a flaming rinse. In pretty pumps
  Betty would hover, carefully, on her bones, greeting
Without addressing them, then fade toward that sweet-hearted
  Heart-beckoning place, alert with lifelikeness,
Where the flours would have been sifted and the quinces cooked
  (Although they never were being done the day one stopped in);
The most the kitchen revealed to its grieving fold, a great
  Corolla of vanilla light, and a sense the fire was cold.
Hard to grasp these emanations as a judgment:
  Emptiness, no less than the tinkling splinters
Of grace, mere emergent gargoyles of the dark. . . .

IV. *All Souls'*

Feathery in movement, all of Betty's handmaids, contrary
  To her rule of scarlet/royal/loden wool, dressed in cream
Blouses and heathery tweed skirts. They were, like her,
  Impeccable with age, and so cheerfully "set out" the inevitable
Flaw in each was clearly framed. One had bloodshot eyes,
  Another a hump, a third fingers turning askew from the knuckles,
Scales in the skin common. Betty indeed had long, tawny teeth
  Chiming eerily with the colors of her costume, and yet
These faint grotesqueries only made to seem more ample and, more, kind
  The pressed pleats and the gentle perfumes and the exact
Touches of face powder that sifted upon the ineffable modesty
  Of the questions and of the persons who blossomed at our bidding.
Their imperfections rose before us in our limbo of aggression
  Like artifices of well-tended realism designed to prove
The women who had no reason to be here were historical beings
  After all, that even in eternity the ruse of the body must appear
Complete. They smiled, a small expectant wistful amused smile,
  Like sweetly groomed children, oh beautifully trained
For display, who for our sakes did so earnestly want to get
  Right these broken and unnatural gestures of the earth.

RINGING WORDS

THEY have closed the prison where they had you teach
The killers no one else would touch. Brutal,
Mercurial, in lessons they would leap
Catlike in a twinkling to the desk
Or throw you to the ground and in distraction
Toy with you, half-sated tigers with
Unappetizing fare, but flanked by foes.

So the last casualties have followed you
Into a daylight too much for their eyes,
The wards and keeps flushed out in back of them.
If many stayed down, tormented by their boredom
To deeps of vehemence not to be calmed,
Bleeding mad, their babble like the birds',
Some died. The walls would crumble around them all.

"Forget," said the voice politic, "that place
Sacramental in the crime it fed
Even as it punished it. Our health
Requires this." Our. Our. My spared limbs
Tremble with a passion the old rue
Will punish later, "Some memorial
Is needed to appall the mind," I said,

"Lest all he had resisted when it mattered
Little any more, loosen like Proteus,
Shrug away its hides, and sink oblivious
To all its harm—yes, feeling the bright blood move,
The freshened sinews round the strengthened bone,
Feeding its stripes into the sea."

THE CHARM

I

As if you were still there within your grid
Of iron catwalks stretched into the dark:
I overhear you from another room
Making a prisoner's sounds, cramping with gas,
Drawing from brittle lungs a string of phlegm
That sounds made out of something corrugated,
Even the savage cough a kind of ritual
To cover the huge empty span
Of creaks and breathings from the snowbound house,
Which you know your presence magnifies,
Dry echo of millennial abrasions
Eking out decay in a settling of grit.

Where you should be, the air is derelict,
Light shut down, shut out, the fuel capped
So only an inkling charges the wires
Bearing on a slender flux of current
To a low-watt incandescent bulb
That won't ask much. It lights your rounds,
Old child doing service to the void,
God, temple, janitor in one, frayed
Dried out body of my worship, swept with age.

II

> "... there is much to be said for the Celtic belief that the souls of those whom we have lost are held captive in some inferior being, in an animal, in a plant, in some inanimate object, and so effectively lost to us until the day (which to many never comes) when we happen to pass by the tree or to obtain possession of the object which forms their prison."
> —Proust

Into what thwarted object have you gone
With your smooth waist and long deliberate gait?
What mask of otherness in ordinary
Usage do you wear so I can't see it,
Can't see you in it? the kindling basket's?—
Do you writhe in desiccated willow,
Your long backbone coiled into a shriek?
Has some boyish tribal object claimed you?—
Toilet kit, worn parka, ring for keys,
The automatic pencil whose thin lead
Was visible through the blue plastic hull?

Odd, how little you had about you then,
How much of it was worthless. Yet you kept these,
In lowerclass bullheadedness and thrift:
I comb through your effects when you are out
Like one bereaved. I keep on calling.

III

Winter has sunk you further down than ever

As if frozen in a talisman
We let slip from us, ignorant of its worth
(Your family sofa? the cheap lamp
Of blue china that blew up in sparks?
The cobalt navy sportscar that was stolen?).

Trapped in the horsehair, dash, or blackened harp,
Fallen deeper in the garbage lot
Among debris trickling with basin clay,
Do you shift compacted under layers?
Embedded with the plants you had no use for
(Preferring your apartments be hygienic)
Must you be torn from the dim toothy briar?
Dug from the meat of the jonquil underground?
Picked through with the shed needles of the fir
Against the urine of the dogs against the snow?
Must I let down my hands, imagining
Evil has charmed the atoms of the starlings
In snow grown hard as brick, the bricks loose powder
That breaks off the buildings like the heads of scabs?

IV

Above my head the frequencies of matter
Wrinkle and flex into a dome of chitin
Clear as empty sky, which I drag with me.
The sudden sun falls with its eager will
Over the gables and flanks of unalterable form.

Nothing ever starts and trembles when
I say your name.

V

Even should I seek you in the books
No longer taken from the even row,
Which struck me as inhuman in their code,
The dazzling workmanship of modern type
Lacing through the integral equation
Or great regimentary matrices,
Serifs like pikestaffs on the horde of numbers
Edging outward in some city's dusk
Until these thick-ranked figures dim, and blacken,
And like a myriad window chinks, drained of their life,
Extinguish by the thousands in perspective
To cubes of ink,
                    I still might imagine down
The vertical axis a shiver straightening
As would a spinal cord and behind the print,
Loosing floods of intermittent darkness
Like a wrong beacon, cosmic wastes through which
Course the tears of your enchanted soul.

VI

You would find this foolish. You are not there.
No one is there. The world is what it is made of,
What we have made it,
What we must suffer
Is just the working of excessive skill
Circling the skull
On substance haunted by its dwindling.

VII

Yet it may end far otherwise. I may be walking
Down the hallway to pick up the baby from her nap
And see the linen closet partway open and from

A stack of clothing folded for Goodwill will come
Whimpering as from a dog who stands up just
Before it has awakened and treads awry on a forelimb

Drained of blood and O God darling in old clothes
There at parade rest hips rocked easily forward
Thighs rounded like long fruit nipped at the knee

Defining the worn planes of the blue jeans you will be
Standing your face lightly stained as by a photographic
Process to a filmy tan your teeth burning your lips also

Burning yet when you make no movement toward me
(Hushed by my will? a magnet silenced by the stream
Of filings that oar constantly toward its cove

Across the ambiguous interval where nothing is
But hurry?), Let him not fade before I come, I say.

To this you will smile from the pale where wish is reason

Where you had been anchored all along and all the past
Fall like glass from the impatient frame, grain,
Splinter, caul quick now and bent to loosen

That transparence where at length the window vanishes
And time pours back glinting atop its deeper basis,
Spray tearing like comets off its black unbroken current.

II. MASKED WOMEN

For my teachers

MASKED WOMAN'S SONG

Before I saw the tall man
Few women should see,
Beautiful and imposing
Was marble to me.

And virtue had its place
And evil its alarms,
But not for that worn face,
And not in those roped arms.

—Louise Bogan

Thirst

DREAD

BECAUSE imprisoned by the mysteries—
Weeping in the middle of the night,
Blue light at dawn that makes the sheet like snow,
Overnight forsythia and flies,
Children's toys surprising as a gunboat
In the alley and (she thought) as loud,
Sport and sweat and blow-by-blow disease,
Chimes that would unnerve the very clouds
That float above denominated spires—
She turned to meet her old desire
To wake into the past, to find beliefs
Uncountable as edges on the leaves.

Sitting up. The horrid day begins,
Its passage nude of meaning though its symbols
Propagate, identical, like greetings
Neither meant. The eggs, the paschal lambs
From springform pans, the rusty hams.
How sorry to be old and to be ill,
To have slept when it was cool,
To know the music heard behind the eyes
Was but the step of agony
Trying to be genial.
We did our best, she thinks; we kept our meetings;
We cannot ease the living of our sins.

The heart breaks to no purpose in the spring.
Memory reopened as desire,
Tulips seem like images or runes
By which to read the night against the day
Or force old happiness, the ragged fire
And blurred demeanor of a summer noon,

To be itself again in promising.
Opening and closing like a cave
Chance is with us to the end, its masks
A banner in the desert, walls that meet,
Climates where one was not meant to breathe
And sweetness like a tyrant in our grasp.

THE BAMBERGER REITER

When he came to her in the night—the great
Muscular smooth god who stroked her flesh,
Patient, unimportunate, with broad

Gold fingertips—testing her faith,
He hung above her complicated life,
Its fuzziness, and started the long plot

Involving things he gave her, those sudden
Properties: thumb rings, dark with garnets,
Bowels (which the god can see), gypsy

Food, poverty, carouse of siblings
(Yes, and offspring) on the smoky stairs,
Back-stoop stones creviced with New Orleans

Moss, betrayal in shadow, candelabra.
His brow and eye were hooped with actor's carbon
In some faces. Then for her reward,

When he had stopped confusing her, in tawdry
Urban terrifying plots, with someone
Else whom she was not and did not want

To be, he came round, a rural lover
Swinging on a gate, or sailing like
Cherubic figures deep into the nave,

Wicked and pure by turns: a sigh of incense
Whispering from far, or, startling her
Nearby with lucid look and round damp hips

Globing her heated touch, a limber satyr.
Abruptly, he was sunken and remote,
Wit or wraith or involuted mind

Making poetry, a grizzled boy
To whom she offers introductory
Sentences in several turgid versions

None of which is right. Her armpits flow.
The temple-monkey god leaps from font
To pew, chiding, rueful, noncommittal . . .

These dreams are meant to be embarrassing;
Abound in failures in the very face of stone;
Accuse by chime; refuse by water to reflect

What she is or expects. These dreams . . . are like this one,
She thinks, nasty with interludes as characters shift,
Gods shrivel, and, after it all, we are usual.

But now, out of nothing proven, deserved, or won,
He comes to her in the form of a dusky arch,
Bent bow, silver span; as fillet

Fading into curl, curls into ruby-clustered
Crown; as hand upon an ancient pommel
Primed for war, he comes—things on his mind—

And, flourishing his horse on the epistle
Side, allows her to mount pluming up.
In this dream's breach of fading space, the knight

Sat a horse that melts into a woman;
The woman rode a world that, lastly, rhymed;
The fiery god spoke, "Yes. You," and she'd come through.

NEREID'S SONG

I HELD you in my arms,
Saying what was true—
Forbidden things, endearments
Someone else had given
Me that all were spent,
An amber lie or two—
I thought, What could this harm?
I thought, that I was driven.

When you harried me
Grimacing long in love
And I but dimly knew
That everybody knew
My shaking fits swept in
And mutely covered me
If you were near: when sin
Galloped through the grove;

When all of this was real
And when your eyes were black
As water in a dream,
When (I say) in you
I saw the mirror's back
And broken silver seal,
How could I mend the screen,
Stride through my gaze to you?

But when the feathered light
Through porch and corridor
Touches in its sweep
Amphora and mouth,

And when we flutter like
Anemones in deep
Gatherings of breath,
The ocean's at the door.

WHEN WE TURNED OUR BACKS ON IT, THE OCEAN

I

LOSING form in the recoiling weather,
Water lapses in the weather tube,
Wives turn tear-streaked faces to the stove,
Objects precious in longevity
(Though bleached in transfer) shatter after all;
Unquiet hearts pull savagely at coats
But do not leave the house—or don't come home.
Pebbles stutter in the grass.
No one plays with them. The children stall,
Disturbing, terrified, but, pale and manly,
Wander down the hall, keep to their rooms.
Dramatically below, where no one sees,
The ordinary good becomes confused:
Fastidious, the beach and sea deal grossly
With each other now in the disgusting squall.

II

The ocean knows its felonies
There at the skirt. Nosing through
Its shed, it has few ways to turn
And cannot travel anywhere.
Central at its least remove,
Its mind can lash across the leagues.
In flaccid moods, its body bare
Of differences, disparities,
The waters brood and burn.
They are our thought; they gave us birth.
What we know fitfully in air

Was once an emerald unity,
Love the same as movement, truth
A torsion in the baptistry
Of tempests where the wave was priest.

III

Subjected to the sky
Ambiguous I ease
From cliff to sacred cove,
Gliding under boats,
Turning in my sleep
The prisoned life below
Like creatures on a wheel.
Dolphin, flounder, eel
Do not resemble me.
I am the colored bow,
Metaphoric eye
On whom the Father, bored
With unity, increases.
Like eternity
We are too remote to die.

IV

In mockery
The way I go
Casts shadows
On the green.
Fruit on trees
Gleams brassily
As I race white-
And gray-boned by.

You know my eye,
Hesperides
Who call to me
With silver strings:
It is black and old.
I am the bitter sea.
You can't love me.

ISEULT OF BRITTANY

REVERSAL in the air,
Conundrums of despair
Whose clues are drops in pressure,
Cold destructive pleasure
Predictable as weather.

A riddle is its form.
Cold means the alarm
It raises in the spring,
Storm the suffering
For which we were meant.

You came upon the waves.
Music touched the mist—
Silvery wet manes
By lightning kissed
As they were driven out to sea.

Now clouds fall in the pool.
The waters turn their face.
No one is to blame.
The earth has cooled
And you and I are dying.

OLD AFFAIR

THE thing seemed cold: His hair
Briary to her eye
Though she had breathed its air
Shaking across the sky.

Hands at their quick stress;—
Limb and flank thrust up;—
Now, in idle dress,
Manage a coffee cup.

The glance coaxing and small,
Skin tightened like horn.
The flesh, sporadical,
Fretted by their scorn.

Not that desire was sick
But that it never was
More than the self's small wick
Sunk in its applause.

MODERN LOVE

HE thrust aside her clothing.
He opened up her flesh,
Broke the nearby mirrors
And shattered all the glass.

He tipped the headless porter.
He tidied up the bed.
He said he didn't love her,
Said he wished her dead.

He found the furthest cavern.
He tried her like a pool
In which the pleasures of the gods
And goddesses are tooled.

He looked into her black eyes.
He looked into his own.
He found a bald identity
That made him murderous.

He tried on all her jewels,
Tore through all her scarves,
Fell upon the travel trunks
And ripped the labels down

From Tulsa and Trieste,
Utrecht and Lissabon,
Then stole from her the voyaging
She had never done.

The morning light no kinder
Than water in the tub

Showed each to the other
Desperate, wan with love.

He held his breath and wandered
Into the restaurant,
Ordered in the local tongue,
Admired the slim patronne.

He listened to her stories,
Told one of his own,
Gave up nothing, took the earth,
And told another one.

Time passes; in corruption
Nightmare follows him
To the hot dead places
They had never been:

There were horses slaughtered.
Maids were being sold.
Trinkets were in evidence,
Spices on the rug.

He looked into her black eyes,
Open like his own,
Took her in his jewelled glove,
Drew the beaded screen,

Used her as it was his wont
To do in any latitude,
Knelt and kissed her up and down
And cast her off for good.

PARTING INSCRIPTION

At the final hour, half beside himself,
Theseus toyed in wax with messages:
Do not grieve, in fact forget
Me on the forecastle here, the sailors beckoning
To lift aweigh. The ocean stretches
Out its listlessly impatient limbs
Among the blemished Cyclades,
The mouth a little dry and dull.
It *looks* indifferent, but bends
Its female will, its very launching surf
And tawdry horizontal eye upon my symmetries.
Sorry. Be in touch. N.B. the faun
Near the acacia shrub, blood in the next room.
You earned it for your greed, my dear,
Or hubris as we call it here.

VULCAN

THE old mechanic at the service station,
Silver before his slowly cancelled fire,
Said he had two at home like her. She told him—
Blue-eyed, bearded, grimy as he was—
That she was getting on. Mercedes-Benz
And Jaguar hummed coolly past, appointed
By him like candescent stars.
Resigned, he helped her through the waiting wall.
They fell together like the snow.

He took her through the windy agora
Of Europe, skirting forgeries in flesh,
Into arcades of cameo and mute faience.
Keeping by him, seeing through his eyes
What he had seen too long—lindens,
Cornices, and pools, staring palaces,
Secretive châteaux, the cities where
He yearned for Picardy and there
Tooled priceless hunting paths to stalk—
She knew she was done in.
Illumined to her bony cord
(Another gem beneath his gaze),
She gave on hollow sky. Their love grew clear
But insurmountable. Turned against him

In the streets she hugs his Dorian neck and weeps.

THE SAME LOVE

THERE is the love that makes you feel
Your life will never end; and then the one—
Embrace of bright mortality
In warm metal come

Between brazen surface and descending lake—
When the voice you could identify from any
Other whispers at your cheek
The old drowning endearments of the many.

Love alters when it finds
That it must mask its reasons as it goes;
With a hard eye
By their less snowfall trace the standing roads;

But lifting a poor brilliance to the glass
Can read no word of how the thirst of love would pass.

Regret

MELISANDE

AWAKENING in the sixteenth century
Was wonderful. I had a hot cross bun,
Brushed the drowsy butterflies away
From the brunette grasses of my early form,
Went to the bar before the mirror and danced
Until exertion was like dew, licked
Reverently away by kings, valets,
Suns of innocence in that pure time.

Summer was of course the season,
Doubtless puberty the task.
I loved my father and my reason.
I loved my mother and my mask.

Gerhardt and Guillaume came by to see me.
Linden rows obscured their doublets' pique
With pikes and shadows of their tossing own.
Half in, half out of rapid turns of light
And leaf, I did *battements en cloche* and left them
To their hounds and money bags and ale.
I stepped toward the meadow with my dog
Named River Man, my cat named Cress.

And then . . . what? This part of the day
Always filled out clumsily. Did I climb
My father's knee, roam my mother's suite?
Lutes I seem to recollect, my brothers'
Formal practice with their blades, tutorials
In one grace and another, daily rain,
Foyers where the servants sunk their teeth
(When no one was about) into a tapestry,
A sombre hawk, a mauling in the wood.

But then came evening. From the casement
I could hear the thunder like a hiss invade
The willows near. We shivered. Clear
Fatedness was to be seen and, heard,
Panels sliding open from behind me.
The world was double then. The room beyond
(One for which there was no brick, no rift,
No sign) was gray, had plaster chains through painted
Iron hoops, but was, in mirror, wooden
Bay, and view of warning willows, like my own.

He sat upon a stool, grammarian
Or envoy from an unseen Italy.
On his lap, the text in cloisonné
From which he reads, each dusk, my versions.
Tropes are tried, tmesis, paradox,
Synecdoche, as I rise up more clean
And insubstantial than a yawn from Cress,
Her panther legs composed upon his knee.
There is neither approbation nor
Belief. I pat the floor in morrices,
Flash like tiny flames, and make a meaning
Of the time between my one turn and
My other but, impassive, unimpressed,
My tutor and my witness turns the page.

Capes, foils, commedia dell'arte dwarves
Interrogatively scamper from
His lips: and from the center of my heart
A leap like the Corsair's begins to bell,
Suspense pulled out to every reaching limb.
Turning to him from my timeless shelf
As paused upon the wave until my bow
Elect its lacy downward slant,
I find him moved but still deliberate.
He holds his place, leans forward; Cress retreats

Into the fading light. "I find in you,"
He says as I come settling to my feet,
"My last and full delight. But we
Need legend and geography—to see
How far you fall, how wide I reach."

He stands quite near me now, lays down the book.
Then bucklers, marble, ermine, orbs,
Raiment of that violence in rule,
Pour in passionate monotony
From his frank and stormy face.
In the spirit of that realm, myself
Elaborate, heartbroken, fully grown,
An arm indicatively cool against
The willows repetitious in the wind,
I rise to classic point, *développer*
À la seconde, hauteur toward the utter
Ceiling of my doom as tears of granted
Definition solve the dimming evening
Mirror into sheets of silver rain.

In the penultimate embrace
Of doubles in the glass, his light,
His shade became my future and
My past, his hands upon my face
A lengthy benison, a seal.

It was the termless sixteenth century.
It would never come to me again.

THE BLUE WOOD

THE place stands on its first foundation.
Plants and flowers—paintbrush, vetch—
Have hardly had their say in soil
Whose flora is ambiguous with age.
The sand about the fieldstone blank
That rests on an uneasy rise
Of lonely insubstantial land
Grows reeds of stubble grass the shade
Of hay, historical, and tired.
No one has ever lived enough;
The forest is never still.

Cartography—no help. "This region.
Rich in waters lanced like bulbs
To one thin northern source. Are muddy-
Bottomed, barely stir, reflect
Their lacy due of surface weather,
Rise compatibly and plummet
By the clock, move cold and brown."

Yet we did live here, cold and true.
The place fell to its first foundation.
Stone like a sleeve against my wrist.
Streams like arrows in the peace.
Your flesh above like destiny
Whose slicing hour never struck
Finale but whose gaze
Spoke axe to glove.

STUNDENBUCH

THE blunt view of the bell tower,
Four iron burdens
That tip four tones—
I have known this landscape by heart.
Angelus. Once rung out
For lepers, mendicants,
Markts, guilds, a pope's
Election, wars and wars. Often
Bombarded for days, they processed
Or were guillotined or bled
To the decorum of bells
In the royal blue zodiac.

My bells are different, heavy;
Are a bit cheap, slow to
Peal and so call forward
Lands of an alien
Earnest good humor,
Of a history so cruelly
Negligible that the sky
Is only mildly moved.

But these bells are practically
Brand new, too. Sundays
They scatter the faithful, covies
Of great-chested ladies, a halo
Of bony gulls shiver—the second
Split like a jagged-off frame
In an old silent.

Sundown then.
Lumbering to a standstill

The four bells drink down
Lips from a spigot of snow.
Beyond them, roofs
Out of a Utrillo echo a matte
Patter in the alleyways. And I?
Could die of thirst
In an air, this pink.

GLAD DAY

SUCH cloudy mornings full of mist
        In papery sheets
    That muffle up the power poles—
The deep and serious gray behind the sky
And permanence of sunless alleyways

    As if dim cover made the lengths
        Of earth more real—
    These are the joys of area.
The little sooty city tests its arms
And twinkling lights, extinguishing at dawn,

    And knows for once its shape and mind.
        Not like the blocks
    Burned into rising definition:
The plucking partiality of light
That puts the whole to quarters and to bits

    And drags up consciousness and self-
        Referring shame.
    Light is so psychological,
Partitioning the humors on a grid
Where each square has a muddy wheel-shaped stain

    That makes it work abashed, apart.
        Shadow equals,
    Soothes, encourages. Benign,
Expressionless, abstracted, thinking of someone
Else, the graying heaven strokes the earth.

PLAGUE SUMMER

Homage to Albert Camus

THE leaden heat beats down on the deadening drum
The dusty town rolls out, wave after wave
Stifling the sea and in delirium
Plunging alike the foolish and the grave.

The dusty town rolls out, wave after wave,
An evening like a golden-reddish shroud,
Plunging alike the foolish and the grave
Into the alien vacuum of a crowd

Which evening like a golden-reddish shroud
Tints with its lurid climate of soft smoke.
Into the alien vacuum of the crowd
Fear passes with the knife beneath its cloak,

Tints, with its lurid climate of soft smoke,
—Is it the drumming of extinguished souls?
Fear passes with the scythe beneath its cloak,
Hooding from our gaze its empty holes.

Is it the drumming of innumerable soles
Timed to the eerie whistling of the plague
Hooding from our gaze its flashing coals
We hear now from a distance, horrible and vague?

Timed to the eerie whistling of the plague
Stifling the sea, and in delirium,
We hear now from a distance, horrible and vague,
The leaden heat beat down on the deadened drum.

THE BRIEF AGAINST PLURALISM

OTHER people tell me what they know
And what they do. They tell me what
Has hurt them here and was removed, or what
Just went away and what a scare they had.
I'm thought to be a blank and speaking
Confidante. They tell me what a wind-
Fall came and, with as clear a conscience, say
The windfall they'd awaited and engaged
To act upon had dropped out of the sky
In mid-flight—wings too green apparently
To fly the whole route toward their expectation.
I am also told, I'm told in fact as if
I were a pool to hold their telling in, that
They will never get well, or that they've gotten
So much better health is just an old
Routine—a habit like the other of never
Getting well. Perhaps other people
Who tell me all of this conflicting news
Have learned to keep their habits, and persevere
In ways, in any ways, in any given
Ways, so long as ways are plural and
They persevere. Perhaps I don't have habits,
Although I persevere. Perhaps I cannot
Lead a plural life, a life in which
Each part bears one mark.
Perhaps my liberality in giving
Up the old, and my singularity
In taking only one way at a time,
Divide me from habits, which in turn
Prohibits me from telling of the wildly
Good and hopelessly bad as though they were
The same. Which finally prohibits me

From being listened to, from being held
As speaker in that empty space where
Others wait as hearers who can hold
(As if they were a pool to hold tales in)
The weight and the liquidity of life,
Of our life, of this given life, of my life
Which was given, which gives, which takes away.

A GUIDE TO FALLEN COUNTRY

LIKE a scaffold thrown
Temporarily against
The broken wall that you must also mend,—
Do not think that you can hold
Beneath eccentrics like the king
Who yanks the world behind him
Down the corridor, nor under dance
Of any sort, nor under
Haunches as displayed
In slumber when you gather head,
Taming and succumbing at a stroke
That in the dream parts hip from thigh.
Do not throw your weight about
But like a thief in your own closet
Sidle through the human clothes
Clinging to their attitudes.
Let nothing move. Be as the tissue
Summer air draws through the trees
At sunset, part element, part shade.
Practice harsh imprisonments.
Draw out your body to the rim; fast
At the periphery; grow thin.
Do not neglect to exercise
The crucial ligaments that translate
Stealthy leap to quiet plank.

Now you may try your reconnoître
Of the structure. Buttresses
Like scimitars will point the way.
Clerestory colonnades still let
The restless searchlights of the day
Scour lopsided aisles in single
File. Incense rises like

Dust from vanished cavalry,
Signifying your omissions,
Grieving never understood,
The valleys of your youth unmapped,
Unreachable, abashed.
The lamps hang webbed in arabesques
Of iron: you recognize this place!—
The Stations where you genuflect
At dusk, the treasons you confess.

Against the missing eastern
Wall, the little huts of rue
Tricked out like an altarpiece,
Draped like chambers are in Poe
Where in the fetid dark you knelt
To stand trial for banality.
Here find the person that you were,
Unregenerate and dull,
Your sign a bank of winter cloud,
Your rosary days of the week,
Your dreams the obvious projections,
Your possessions ordinary.
Out of these what good could come
Beyond the gift for suffering?
Confessors of authority
Like planets in the morning sky
Beckoned you to be and do,
Exemplified eternity
That came and went like Lucifer
On the vague silk of pools.

Beneath the disappearing nave
Worn stone displays the women you
Could never be, butterflies
Of laughter, point, and probity
Beneath whose wings the sudden forests
Fluttered into leaf. They beat

In recollection to your pulse,
These buried queens whose crypts you skirt
Unsteadily like ocean lanes,
The floor a sea of effigies,
Homaged, sovereign, and deep.

And near the empty monstrance, naked
Of the Presence like a light
Gone out, you meet what was undone.
Children you have never had
With hair as thick and straight as rain
And blue-black as the panther's
Pad swiftly breathing "Elohim"
As they fall and rise to harmonies
That once were heard by Jacob at Beth-El.

TO GOD WHO GETS AWAY WITH THINGS

For Ruth Limmer

LET it be gray, Gesù, always.
Let afternoon lose hold,

Azalea shed its tropic tone,
Plaster come to stone.

Let leaves come pasted by the rain
Against abandoned autumn panes.

Allow us linens bleached by time,
Pulse upon the arm,

Hair that settles in the wind,
Putti on the sill.

Fill the bevelled glass with wine.
Crystal's ordinary art

Is hot, then civilized.
Increase the dark, then. Save

The rest of us who cannot speak
But arch and grieved.

Promise what we have to fear
Is what we've always feared.

Give us weather we can see
And grace to leave.

The Gorgon

PAINTING

As Imagined Land this river town
Had everything from spire, volcanic vineyard,
Purple peak as barricade for trade,
To fallow field, traffic on the water
And in the very palace porphyry,
Brown marble, tile, smoked glass, the willing tithes
Of every craft and earthly century.

Here is no refusal of design,
Much more its faintly old-world apogee
As, even then, those who had made their peace
Should cast with an alert and pleasant eye
Back to the childhood of their present faith,
Recall the tokens of a godless time
Conscripted in the penmanship of plan.

That she wore velvet deep as Tyrian,
Brocade he lush as landscape in a dream
Was the point. The muses of reaction
Knew they must intoxicate the eye
To lay the conscious rigors of the sense.

Yet how quietly the jewels of the border
Of the Virgin's gown, around the crystal orb
The Christchild cradles like a careful toy
Absorb the light, unhurried, descending
From an inner source we cannot turn to see:

The Father pacing at His endless Office
Pauses to approve His lighted scene:
Sky before a storm or shortly after

Casts its milky way upon the Meuse,
And motionless the world, and still the servants
Roam about with nothing much to do
And peacocks sweep the lilies with their tails.

GHIBERTI'S EVE

Eastern Door, "The Gates of
Paradise," set in place in 1452

RISING from a bas relief in Eden
The finest naked thing in all the age,
A half-round Eve unseen as yet by Adam.

God holds her wrist and sadly courts her gaze,
His blessing hand hypnotic and benign,
A slender, careworn Christ in middle age.

The space between them is her long arm's line.
These are the first of faith's Enamored Ones.
The last meet in the narthex, palatine

Yet gothic, where Sheba's pledged to Solomon.
All the panoply that intervenes
But brought God's distance to a minimum.

That is part of Paradise, it seems,
To start so far away yet end so near,
With one relation taken to extremes.

Eve drew on all his wisdom to compare:
Smooth as a dolphin, grave as Magdalene,
Taut in color as the morning air;

Bright yet dense as good analogy,
Her body strong as undefined desire
And framed in darkness as what one believes—

Accessible thereafter to despair
That's apt to spread on sudden rags of wind
Whenever fire approaches to the fire

Or deliberation to the chance of sin—
Presently she will come to: a sense
Of time in place, dark burning in the limbs

About whose lightning arc four winged infants,
Doves and sparrows, float at her debut.
One combs her hair with his short fingers.

One offers her right elbow to bon Dieu.
One clasps her other arm and hides behind it.
The last one steadies her round womb.

Hovering like birds, they speak like angels,
"Here, my Lord, she comes to you,"
But cannot quite look up to see the Maker.

"Here," they sing, "she's shy, she's new.
Her elbows are all rivery.
She's half-awake and white as dew.

"Her hair smells like the trees
And not like me and not like you.
Warm is everything about her knees

"And neck and miracle, here," the angels croon
Above whom leaning spirits in a crescent
Fold their soft small arms: for them this view

Was all the universe was meant
To do, this sleeping man whose dream they guarded,
Mermaid, King, and swimming firmament.

But by the time he drives them from the garden
God is old and wears a magic hat,
Bangs his stick and says he's tired of them,

While on the currents at his mystic back
Fullgrown naiads ripe and long as Eve
Gaze down on earth as loath to leave all that,

And one looks long upon the rustling pomegranate tree.

THE BETROTHED

Clerks and Spaniards at the door
Beg alms of me or that I lend
Some lustre to their brazen tales.
Next door the king is at his lathe
With studs and gimlets, making traps
To fool the devil as the mice
Are fooled by heathen bait.
Antique, turbaned, and intent,
A husband in the fearful lapse
Eternity tucks into life,
He fashions me a tiny grate
To fit a stool to warm my feet
While I read on in this cold century.

The candle just went out. No fire
Warms the hearth. I am reading prose
From gilt, historiated
Pergament. The angel has come
Again, wings like dark pontoons.
He kneels as usual, brow aglow
Beneath his small tiara. Wire
Crosses in the sun, the moon-
Shaped windows that repeat his face,
Wicker, grill—all perforate
With meaning in a foreign tongue,
Messages I cannot read—
Derange my conscience, plant the seed.

What he announces, or but tries,
Fumbling with the shining ivory
Syllables that fall like banners
Or like weightless curls of paper

To the mosaic *verso* of the floor,
Is an old cosmology,
I think, related to this vast
Retreat of alternating tiles—
As in his zodiac, where stars
Nightly loose their hold on caelar
Concords, perspectival manners.
He frames my life in lilies and election,
Lunettes that harbor sky by its defection.

Everywhere I go, he waits.
I step outside. Our stair is worn.
The garden is in disrepute.
A dove is hovering in chains.
Bereft the statuary niche
Where something godly would ensue.
"I am the Princess of Mérode,"
I say. "On one side I am Gothic,
On the other odalisque.
I coveted the very risk
That fell from language into thorn,
About my breast the feathered close
Of alien longing, heretical
Angelic one who calls himself Flémalle.

"Now I must ask of you more art.
Put off the swan, the ring of stone
And liquid tongue so like the spheres'.
Close up the panel where the old
King fidgets in his sleep.
Save me from the ancillary
Legends reaching backward from
The very air I breathe. Hear
What I say not what I seem:

It aches beneath my heart.
I am too late, too clear, too bold
To live by liturgy."

"Then you shall have him man, as mortal cast.
And you shall love him like my first, your last."

AN ENGRAVING OF BLAKE

FROM the ceiling near the roof
Runs the smoke of star and field:
The father brings his weather proof
That he will try, and we will yield.
The bolt unwinds into the dark;
His beard is blowing in the dark.

About his eyes, no energy.
The climate falls into his hand.
We cast about us as we sleep
And see, that this is as he planned—
That we should know his earth, his air
For rocks of tears, and rivers of hair.

CHAGALL IN HIS SICKNESS

WHEN we came to the darkened town you sang a song
Personal with shadow. I did not mind
Your rural virginals nor goatish strong
Amusement, but my legs still throbbed from the pine
Spires and red chimney brick. You made a sign
To me (we were circling near the Vilna fair)
That I would not be harmed by flame- or rime-
White leaves, blue violins, grief at the bier,
Nor by the golden tallow that was falling everywhere.

The sky was sharp with fires and fiddle bows.
Soaring cocks let down their ladders in the blue.
Green crucifix and blue Redeemer grow
From pikes and handstands: juggling seems to you
Like pain, or revolution will prelude
In fracas, certainly, but at the cool
Center of the milling wrists, a Jew
Nods; the ass sits on the milkmaid's stool;
One happy Russian upsidedown as humans do

Not do (not on one arm! nor rocking clear
Upon the chancy air above the samovar!)
Defies along his Lenin lines the gear
Of minstrelsy, on one hand, brandished spar
And cudgeled dead among the tabernacular
Detritus on the left. The wall clocks wear
A languid look, a player's golden tabor
Lures him to the winking sky, but there
Is that old table with the Torah for his care.

Saltimbanques, grotesques, equestriennes,
Voyageurs, and Saints Voituriers
Bound, kick, and stride, make S's, daleths, bend

To holy and betraying earth. Today
When we were married there were children on my cheeks.
When I was Mary there were icons in my womb.
When I was Bella there were angels at my beck,
Clouds in my room. And when we strolled my lip
Lay tender on your ankle, your arms embraced my feet.

Now when we float into the peopled sky
He draws me up the saddle to recline
Among the tendrils of my gown. Warming we twine
Over upon his form. I kiss the liquid eye,
The comb and gentle beak. His withers press
My tiny spangled breast. A permanent cry
Starts from our mouths above the town
Whose guardians we are, yet looking down
We find the world grows childish with a lost excess.

ON THE ACTOR EDWARD PETHERBRIDGE

I. *In 'Nicholas Nickleby'*

In that dark place of bodies and bodily gloom,
He seemed the source of light, floating his hand
In a sweet consternation of costume,

The outer man a secret firebrand
Of inward work sustained in ravishment
At our good luck, who could not understand—

This in his odd gait was evident
And in his ravaged addled childlike gaze
As of a saint forgetfully intent

Upon the truth—why life made castaways
Of plain folk who shone specially, like ourself.
We see him his long elbowed arm upraise

To make this point then earnest lose itself
In the fixation of a fright so keen
It soon made him forgetful of himself,

As if the actor could reject the scene
Of strut and kitsch and feigning that were not
Different, either, from what he strove to mean.

Still, every eye was on him when he brought
His breath out in a golden sort of sigh
Both sad and small, and heatedly inwrought,

And for all that, as I look back, distantly dry.

II. *In the Role of Lord Peter Wimsey*

These qualities of soul blend curiously,
In the star role, with a breathtaking sex.
Nobody before had gone so high

Into that register, a circumflex
Of joy above the dottiness and crust
Wimsey was groomed for, his manners so complex

And civilly so languid that they must
Have taken centuries of the worst kind
Of noble to bring home their suaver thrust.

But in this last son, witty from war, rich, kind,
All the decorum glided into place,
Each sad quirk true; each generous gesture blind;

And over all, a pilgrim's fretful grace
Heavy with unfulfillment and old rue
As Harriet like a soul before him sways.

Edward as Peter wishes to undo
Her tangle, with his body her extent
Long worship and wise taste and fair renew,

To fade with her in strict dishevelment
As if to augment what he suffered of
With eros deep in being patient.

How like the moment when, in the tale, Great Love
Speaks the one promise of the heart: "Come. Live
Fraught with dark fire, brimming over of

Earth's sweetest good—strength, wealth, what faith can give.
Sit. Listen to my story. Watch my lips.
You need but look into my eyes to live."

So in the end we do. We watch the screen and live.

III. *Dorothy in Edward's Light*

Half knowing Vergil's lesson that all love
Flares up reflexive, of itself unquenchable
Until the best will, winnowing from above,

Put ill out, for me the art is flammable
He practices.
                    Insolent longing brent
No less the author of long notes on hell,

Illusion, and self-love, her late life spent
Translating what in Dante's counter-art
Was sin, but in her own replenishment.

In love with her production from the start,
Obsessed with his serene embodiment,
How hard it seemed to quell what he would start

Once the stirred up senses swooned down to the heart.

THE HUMAN FACE

After seeing Herzog's *Kaspar Hauser*

A FILM of green, unfocused plush, of fantasy,
A thing ill done and temporally coy
Whose script was full of plotting flaws,
Obligatory types, and reconnoîtres
In the village, straw, amusement tent,
On hillside and cobbled *Gasse*. And parables
So crippled by self-evidential wisdom
That one wished for Sufis at the doors
Who could lead us to their mystic schools
And tell us how to tell their lives in tales.

Barring such improbable improvement
In us or films we have just seen through,
There was a recompense in *him:*
An unformed actor with a face like Caritas
Gazing unmoved and meditative on something
Not to be borne for degradation—no deluding
Trick of bone or plane of pumiced skin
For light and camera to flash off on.
This actor was a mime from some antique
Conversion, long lost now, who played in blood
To mad and violent men the role of love
That does not flinch at murder, fire, contumely,
But is, in deep self-recognition, kind.

We live in a careering age,
Importuned by the human faces
Opened upon our own, eating us down,
Entreating us to take them nakedly—
Their eyes, dieted on their own derision,
Still hot for what to tear.
From time to time, a distant recognition

Of the sin we sin—the sacrilege
Of far too many beautiful, irregular,
Real faces blithely shown—will make us halt,
Erase our pleasure, loose the ancient terror
That we have lapsed too far as sybarites
In a cult whose priests are evil, and mute as we.
We have lost the gift of reading what we see.
We look on gods and think them "interesting."

The world was not contrived to be perspicuous.
In a pocket of the conscience, we believe
The human face inviolable and hidden:
The bones that move on secret knob and hinge
Under this remarkable featuring of the tissues.
The autonomic blink and smile. The nude
And primitive forehead scored by intent.
The horrible deep nose whose meaning
Is both arc and refuse and which disappears
Head on. That disappearance. Angles. Moods.
The will of skin about the mouth to wound,
To torture and subdue. And then the sense
Of mouth for voice. Moisture that composes
Temple, brow, and the idea of reach.
The glazing elasticity of flesh.
The chin at solemn structural rest in bone.
The secret and misgiving pool of eye.
The face whom none can dare to say is thing
That is lost being. The one none dares portray.

Accidie

ALLEGORY

WEARING her iron face
Framed by colorless hair,
Astraea haunts the fair
Abandoned common place.

She must draw out the little
We still feel (soon to be null),
Or, as we harden, fade,
Transmuting her own footstep—
The last of the gods to leave.

Heaven watched her as the day drew on.
She could not breathe. The ivy browned beneath
Her feet while night clung masklike to her lids
And webbed her tongue. Reasons left their words.
Speech fell to ruins of abstract
Entablature. Stock-still monoliths
Bore legends at their base she could not read,
Angular and dark like honeycomb,
A diacritical geometry
Whose paeans and exceptions had no key.

Attend, the shepherds whispered to their mates
(This reached her as their compact to *amend*
As they embraced among the pleated ferns),
Her waxy eye upon us, stumbling verdicts
On the new, her yearning sentences
Of rectitude!

When, maddened from the wood
She strode, transformed, serene, contemporary,
Emerald serpent at her feet, moons in her curls,
The wrinkled man-god at her beating breast,

Then, calm and bored (they had seen it all before),
The gods relaxed at her virginity,
Agreeing she had become enough like them
They need not banish her among the stars
And could erase her dark night from the stones.

THE MUSE OF SATIRE

THEY put her together out of this and that.
Skins of tiny pears made up an elbow.
Often kissed, the silky arch of someone
Else's brow. Laid like the narrow glove
Rich relatives have fondled, a brown hand
Of hair upon the knee cast forward from
Her bowed, transparent head. A rumpled breast,
Bricks showing through her half-completed navel,
A brace to keep her lavish sex in place
Round out the sketch. Temporarily, a working draft
Of pain. In time, perfected so she never
Walks again, she'll burn your buildings down.

MEETING THE FAMILY

I HAVE scenes with a mother, not mine.
Nothing's mine. The home I've yet to see
Has a mantel sprouting wonders: a Chinese
China punch bowl—milky leaf
Of porcelain bone rolling
With gauze blue scholars
Whose sandals tinkle through the pane
Of womanish hieroglyph. Moose
Antlers burst from mirrors. It is
My entrance that should shatter
A usable history, a rug pattern.

Their own Orient crowds (enormous bulls
With untold sex and fearsomeness)
Upon the cushioned corners. An unlit
Five o'clock wince of aged glare
Holds at the windows. And over a breakable
Crystal heart, the cherryprint chest
Of my unmet mother awkwardly moves:
"Duckling," "Squirt," or "Dearie,"
She calls me. One word, perhaps,
Exists to mend the three for all time

Into a whole of wrath, banality, and love
Like meditations on the empty Taoist hub.

THE PREGNANT SON

In the time of year when budding
Makes the trees sore, the pregnant son
Carries about his tasks his mother's baby—
Really it is her grandchild.
Like a crone in a fairy book,
His silent little cook, small as a bird,
Has quickened him with yeast and oil
And nutmeats she herself will not eat.
She lives in the hot season on his heat.
(When she looked on the cones of lilac blooming,
They turned brown and papery.)

Watchful
Behind the black deeps of the windows
Flecked with reflections, a caged
Bird with her tongue cut out, she has never
Learned to read the imprint of an alien
Claw on the seed-floor of her cell.
Nor has he caused her a moment's flutter.
He hearkens to her while he does the wiring
Of the garden so that lamps of smoky green
Glow within the cypresses and *strobus nana* pines.
But though he listens so hard the light hurts,
Nothing changes in his understanding.

It is as if he could not see the basket
Of his midriff surging up with fruit.
Along the low ridge of the pectorals,
His breasts look rather pretty, broad and short,
But he has never touched them wondering,
Will they flow? —not with that head
Square as a toy's, gray hair lopped
Like a soldier's, even his ears dark

With intemperate exertion. For pleasure,
He drives his long cars roughly
Down his end of the sky,
Raising coils of dust. He cannot seem
To shed his doldrums (day
With no end, man with little friend).

In the spirit's long summer,
Nothing stirs but repetition. Incurious,
The pushy sparrows come and go,
Beaks bright on rubbish
For the private nest. His mother
Lives on straw and heat. Does she, dead
Well-spring, seed-bed, soften
When he holds above the rigid ground
The fitting of the garden hose
From which fall the ecstatic loops
And lisping fans of wide reflective water,
White-gray, then clear-dark,
With which he slakes the earth?
Does she, too, wait
For the rain to course down
On their burning place? Or when her root
Is stirred, will the long plaits
Of wood twine up into stairs
Ending at a gnarled turret
From which the growing child will see
Fowl and deer darting in freedom
Close enough to smell?

                                        On days of rain, the son
Nails up the trellises ribbed like a forest
Tomatoes reddening with moisture
Will dangle from—cool mouths
To press to his large teeth before the cauldron
Breaks them down. Like Joseph
The Carpenter, blind to the truth,

He drives down in the wood his coins
Of wet, striking the nails so the grain
Bends away from the blows—like pressed
Grass, like dead Christ dragging away
From the cross or weeds weighed
By fathoms of taciturn sea.

Yet behind that ring of spray and family fall
Of the small hammer on the hesitant wood no
Fountain whispering of life, no hidden web
Of bells plucked by the breeze make this
A Paradise; no coo of dove
Withstands the siren sigh of the saw
Taking down in the distance a futile tree
Whose stump another engine is engaged
To claw into a golden pulp
Picked over by the glistening beetles long
Its parasite, whom its gases drug;
Nor does hurt in the stricken timber
Groan out above that sound
In the back of all sound, out
On the highway coating the world
With a tearless chalk, where the airhammers
Cough and detonate,
Rending the hardened earth. These,
I think, are what he goes to see,
Tearing his cars over the white flints
Of hurrying cloud.

ACCIDIE

The sin of sloth

THE light, robust buildings
Stand by sand. New. Empty.
Gray roots of banyan-looking trees
Twist their naked loops in and out
The colorless ground as worn as a marble stair.
Thick air, even land, and the sense of cage
Or of embankment make this like a European
Zoo, a monkey island where the terrain
Is memorized by use. It could be
Southern Europe. Lizards on the sill
Flick their dry tongues.
We can hear the enamelled rustle
Of shiny clicking palm fronds overhead.
Darkly leaded panes bell to the dust,
Subaqueous as Gaudi, with amphibian plumb.
A puzzle to the blond, trod earth.
Dull bluish tracks lie in shallow beds
And cross uncontrollably at the horizon.
Here is the switchyard where the day
Has paused at noon.

Everyone
Is cordial and dresses in twill, moiré,
Or faille, blue-black or cream. Some dance.
English is spoken. We become thirsty
And perhaps our last meal
Was hurried, meager, mutable.
Some collars are open. My step is feat.
Verbs fly away from my query,
One I am compelled to put
In their alien tongue: the trains
Point always in a prevailing line

So I let several go.
We wait on the siding, gloved,
A rolled sleeve or two, and watch
The burial. State occasions
Are informal here. Bright shovels ring
Against the obstinate mark.

SUPERBIA

The sin of pride

THEY'VE loosed the Opposites who throng
The middle air, and Antichrist.
He phoned last night, pretending to be you.
He begged to know, How much I wanted him?
What I wanted (or wanted him) to do?
What could I say except, Thy Will?
What promise but, Blood Fealty?
He claimed to have been dreaming of me,
His whisper private, registers awry.
I counselled him to run from dreams
That made our yearning's fruitless outcomes
False, the pain therein too true.
We spoke for hours in the snowy light
Of four o'clock. Come hither love,
I moaned, to me. Were you asleep,
He asked, in bed my dear? Oh did
I waken you? I said, disconsolate,
Can it be you, my real, my mythical
Gold magus, rugged knight? If true,
Why call in secret of a sudden?
Why lounging in a public room
With gray pianos? . . . what is wrong with you? —
Although I knew that I was wrong with him,
The love was missing me, and blue.
But with the sagesse of the centuries
He told me, For each act there is
An onset; for each sin the first descent.
I faltered; I believed in adoration
Not in evil exercise, the cloudy
Lark. This tone was weird, he hadn't breathed
My Christian name nor said a simple thing
Particular to what we lug around

In memory for years (venetian blinds,
Wistaria, the sparrow on the sill)
Without which we are fluent, but unreal.
But he remembered nothing wholly trivial.
When out of character he launched into
Another aching round of tenderness
That sounded read from some bad deed—
Because at last his droning voice,
The sexual monotony, was
Unsavory, unchoice—I cried,
Who are you finally? He paused,
Dear, how drunk and stupid do you
Think I am? and disappeared.

The next calls made me tremble,
Which I refused to answer
(And he would never place).
It was, I fear, an excellent
Wrong number, blotted from the book.

THOSE WHO WILL NOT COME

THOSE who will not come
Are whom I did not see
Before they died—the keys
To their extinguished prophecies.

Nights I might have changed
The arc of the behavior
Of each living thing
As it tried the door.

Nights I would not have
With who won't come again
To tell me I was vile,
An eye still on my smile.

THE PROVISO

EVEN in melancholy overlooked
By a crude censor,
She was natural only when she wrote
Hard with the pencil,

Scratching down a thing, scratching it out,
Hardly two words sparing
In a row, until great verb, mute adjective—
Implore, or *lenient,*

Distillates of traits that were not hers,
Pure, extreme, ample—
Were all that stood before her reverence
As in a temple.

Then came the gift she had not fevered for
That seemed to warn her
She would have to give it up, to use it.
The same old sorrow

That, having not been chosen by the muse,
She must go hobbled,
Grieved her as she studied the few stars,
Consumed with setting.

STORM PICTURES

VISITATION of wind
Against watery boulders,
Tearing at the gray sod—
Into the premature thaw
Lift the coils of hair
From my face planed with darkness,
Whiter than the rock breakfront.

In a span of minutes
As I hold the heavy child
With the familiar gaze,
I have reached all my ages,
The camera loosing
Springs of light
Beneath the net of years.

★

        From this time
Spores of disease
Jarred into exile
Flare out in far households
Like myriad trashfires
In scorched earth.
                    The prince is dead.
The earth heaves him out
Half decayed.

DAY OF BLOOD

RAIN hurries out of the cloud
Bursts along the eaves
Fries on the metal of the flue.

Undulating sky white and brown
Darkened tin mounted on
Lead with steel and glass—

Until the sparse floor
Of the shining clay is
Shot with incandescence . . .

Deeper the tarnish of gore
And coagulating ink
Grief and Love distractedly
Smudge into another
Hieroglyph of torment

As they revise the placement
Of the limbs swathing
Flaps of skin against
Glistening bone
In leaves of linen
Emulsion acrylic photograph

Their hands moving over
The orbs of the eyes
And the organs exhausted
By death the feet
Twisted by the journey
Over the field

So they are small as a child's.

His head is huge and muddy.
On the ground beneath his neck
Grains of ghostwheat
Sewn with paste
Send out the tendrils
Of longitude over the torn world
Which his wife flushes with rain.

SOULS

THE mist is everywhere, like cloth.
We watch a woman with a band
Of children go from house to house,
The daylight running out like sand.

As the last child dawdles out of sight,
A leaf against a blur of leaf,
The cold sinks forward from the west,
Upholding its hard mask of grief.

Then every view is huge with it:
An ancient pity settles back
In us, like an exotic drink
That makes it sweet so much to lack.

Forlorn together, we grow warm
With the exhaustion of the task—
Never to look for clemency,
Never, above all else, to ask.

NOTES

At Wentworth-by-the-Sea, *Pastorale,* "'Make me neat! Make me neat!'": The exclamation of the fey, excitable child Paulina, too small to tie her own sash, in Charlotte Brontë's novel *Villette,* 1851. *Et Excrucior* (title): "And I am in torment." The conclusion of Catullus's epigram "Odi et amo."

Ground Zero (title): "The point on the surface of land or water at, or vertically below or above, the centre of the burst of a nuclear weapon." *Jane's Dictionary of Military Terms,* 1975.

Knight and Death, "as Nero asked Lucan": "Only a short thread is left me/ but I hope I'll be able to dedicate/ my humble songs to the next tyrant./ He won't ask me to cut my veins/ as Nero asked Lucan. He will want/ spontaneous praise gushing from a grateful/ heart and will have it in abundance./ All the same I shall be able to leave/ a lasting trace. In poetry/ what matters is not the content/ but the form." Eugenio Montale, "A Poet," *It Depends, a Notebook of Four Years,* 1977, trans. G. Singh.

Requiem, I. *Christmas,* "as in memories,/ Each existed in a substantive and eternal way": "All around (this Averroes felt also) stretched out to the limits of the earth the Spanish land, where there are few things, but where each seems to exist in a substantive and eternal way." J. L. Borges, *El Aleph,* 1957, trans. James Irby.

Dread: In memory O.G.K. 1898–1977.

Painting: Van Eyck's "Madonna of Nicholas Rolin," 1435.

On the Actor Edward Petherbridge, III. *Dorothy in Edward's Light* (title): Dorothy Sayers, eminent Dante scholar and translator, and author of the Lord Peter Wimsey / Harriet Vane detective romances. "Vergil's Lesson": Dante, *Purgatorio* XVIII.

Allegory: "At the approach of such a period [of social corruption] poetry ever addresses itself to those faculties which are the last to be destroyed, and its voice is heard, like the footsteps of Astraea, departing from the world." Shelley, *A Defence of Poetry,* 1821.

Day of Blood, "his wife": Isis. The painting-collage of which the poem speaks is Anselm Kiefer's "Isis and Osiris," 1986.

BIOGRAPHICAL NOTE

Mary Kinzie was born in 1944 in Montgomery, Alabama. She attended college in Ohio then studied at the Free University of Berlin and Johns Hopkins. She has assembled critical books on Borges and on American little magazines as well as editing collections of contemporary poetry. In addition to extensive poetry reviewing, she has published essays and monographs on a number of lyric and descriptive poets. Her first volume of poems, *The Threshold of the Year,* won the Devins Award. She is also the recipient of a Guggenheim Fellowship in Poetry.